AMP™ QReads™

Level C

PEARSON
AGS Globe

Shoreview, Minnesota

AMP™ *QReads*™ is based upon the instructional routine developed by **Elfrieda (Freddy) H. Hiebert** (Ph.D., University of Wisconsin—Madison). Professor Hiebert is Adjunct Professor at the University of California, Berkeley and has been a classroom teacher, university-based teacher, and educator for over 35 years. She has published over 130 research articles and chapters in journals and books on how instruction and materials influence reading acquisition. Professor Hiebert's TExT model for accessible texts has been used to develop widely-used reading programs, including *QuickReads*® and *QuickReads*® *Technology* (Pearson Learning Group).

The publisher wishes to thank the following educators for their helpful comments during the review process for *AMP*™ *QReads*™. Their assistance has been invaluable:

Shelley Al-Khatib, Teacher, Life Skills, Chippewa Middle School, North Oaks, MN; **Ann Ertl,** ESL Department Lead, Champlin Park High School, Champlin, MN; **Dr. Kathleen Sullivan,** Supervisor, Reading Services Center, Omaha Public Schools, Omaha, NE; **Ryan E. Summers,** Teacher, English, Neelsville Middle School, Germantown, MD.

Acknowledgments appear on page 176, which constitutes an extension of this copyright page.

ISBN-13: 978-0-7854-6304-7
ISBN-10: 0-7854-6304-6

1 2 3 4 5 6 7 8 9 10   11 10 09 08 07

1-800-992-0244
www.agsglobe.com

CONTENTS

Science

Arts and Culture

Social Studies

Literature and Language

Welcome to QReads™!

Please follow these steps for each page of readings:

FIRST READ

1. Read the Fast Facts and think about what you might already know about the topic. Look for two words that are new or difficult. Draw a line under these words.

2. Read the page aloud or silently to yourself. Always include the title at the top of the same page. Take as much time as you need.

3. Find the first page in Building Connections. Write some words or phrases there to help you remember what is important.

SECOND READ

1. Listen and read along silently with your teacher or the audio tracks.

2. Use the target rate of 1 minute when listening and reading along.

3. Ask yourself, what is one thing to remember? Answer the Key Notes question to help find what is important.

THIRD READ

1. Now, try to read as much of the page as you can within 1 minute.

2. Read silently as you are timed for 1 minute. Read aloud with a partner or your teacher. Circle the last word you read at the end of 1 minute.

3. Write down the number of words you read on the page. Review in your mind what is important to remember.

4. Complete the questions or other reading given by your teacher.

Exercise and Your Body

Your body works harder when you exercise.

Fast Facts

- A female weightlifter set a new world record by lifting about 401 pounds.

- The fastest man in the world ran 109 meters in less than 10 seconds.

- In 2001, a man swam about 313 miles and set a world record for nonstop swimming.

What Happens to Your Body?

You're out of breath. You're sweating. Your heart is beating quickly. Your legs feel heavy. These things are happening[24] because you're exercising. Your level of activity has gone up, and these responses are your body's way of dealing with that[45] increased activity level. What's more, these responses are helping your body become more fit.[59]

When you exercise, your body's systems work harder, allowing you to raise your level of activity. Exercise helps you[78] develop a stronger heart and stronger lungs and muscles. If you exercise several times a week, you can get your body into shape.[101]

KEY NOTES

What Happens to Your Body?
What happens when you exercise several times a week?

_____

_____

Exercise and Your Body

Stretching keeps the body flexible.

Fast Facts

- Babies have 350 bones, but some bones fuse, so adults have only 206 bones.

- More than half of the body's bones are in the hands and feet.

- The smallest bone in the body, which is smaller than a grain of rice, is in the ear.

Exercise and the Skeleton

Exercise helps parts of your body that you never see. For example, exercise helps your skeleton, the frame of bones in your body.[27]

Stretching when you exercise can help keep your skeleton flexible. When you stretch, you keep your body from getting[46] stiff. You can also bend and twist better, which means you are more flexible.[60]

Exercise such as walking is also good for you because it helps your bones stay strong, making them less likely to break.[82] In order to keep your whole skeleton flexible and strong, you need to exercise your arms and back, too.[101]

KEY NOTES

Exercise and the Skeleton
What are two ways to keep the skeleton flexible?

_____

_____

Exercise and Your Body

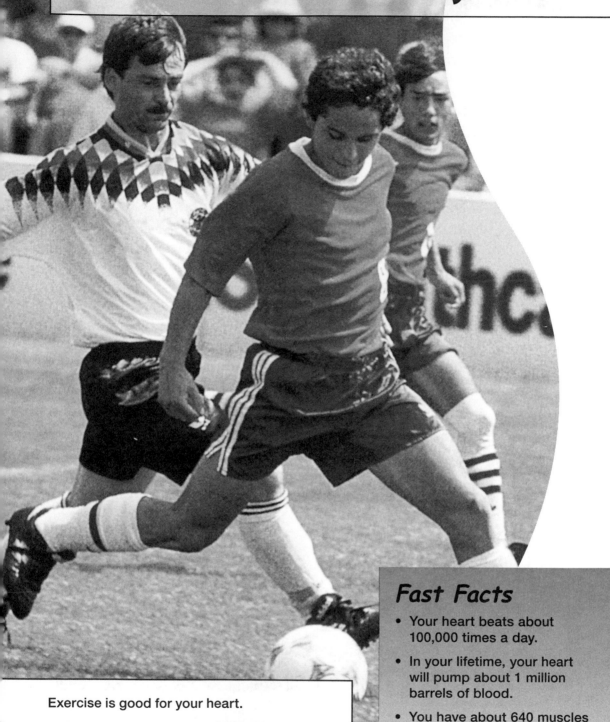

Exercise is good for your heart.

Fast Facts

- Your heart beats about 100,000 times a day.

- In your lifetime, your heart will pump about 1 million barrels of blood.

- You have about 640 muscles in your body.

Exercise and Muscles

As you exercise, you begin to breathe heavily. That's because your muscles are telling you to feed them. What the[23] muscles need is oxygen to do their work, and people get oxygen by breathing it in.[39]

As we breathe, oxygen enters the lungs and then the heart, where it is pumped to the muscles that need it. This activity helps the muscles work better and become stronger.[70]

Exercise helps one very important muscle grow stronger: the heart. When you exercise, your heart works harder. People[88] who exercise develop hearts that are better at one important task—pumping blood.[101]

KEY NOTES

Exercise and Muscles
How does exercise help your muscles?

_____

_____

Exercise and Your Body

Water replaces the liquid lost by sweating.

Fast Facts

- Sweat is 99 percent water and 1 percent wastes and fat.

- The body has from 2 to 5 million sweat glands.

- When you exercise, you can lose more than 2 quarts of liquid an hour by sweating.

Exercise and Skin

You're in the middle of a long run when you see liquid on your skin. It's nothing to worry about. That liquid is sweat, one of the body's responses to exercise.[34]

When you work hard, your body gets warm. Your brain then tells your body to produce sweat. The harder you exercise and the hotter it is, the more you need to sweat.[66]

As the sweat on your skin evaporates, your body cools down. Because of this evaporation, people who exercise need to make[87] sure they drink enough liquid, especially water, to replace the liquid they lose when they sweat.[103]

KEY NOTES

Exercise and Skin
What is sweat?

_____

_____

Exercise and Your Body

What Happens to Your Body?

1. Another good name for "What Happens to Your Body?" is _____

    a. "Kinds of Exercise."
    b. "The Body's Systems."
    c. "The Body's Responses to Exercise."
    d. "Planning an Exercise Program."

2. What are three ways bodies respond to exercise?

_____

_____

_____

3. How does exercise help the body?

_____

_____

_____

Exercise and the Skeleton

1. What is the skeleton?

_____

_____

_____

2. The main idea of "Exercise and the Skeleton" is that _____

    a. you should stretch before you exercise.
    b. exercise helps your heart.
    c. exercise helps your skeleton.
    d. walking is good for your skeleton.

3. What does being *flexible* mean?

_____

_____

_____

Exercise and Muscles

1. People who are exercising breathe heavily because _____

    a. they need more oxygen.
    b. they need to drink more.
    c. they are hurting their body.
    d. they need to make their muscles work.

2. How does oxygen get to the muscles?

_____

_____

_____

3. People who exercise have stronger hearts because _____

    a. they are better runners.
    b. their hearts pump blood better.
    c. their bodies use oxygen better.
    d. their bodies can replace water better.

Exercise and Skin

1. "Exercise and Skin" is MAINLY about _____

    a. why your body sweats.

    b. how to exercise your skin.

    c. why you should keep from sweating.

    d. how exercise helps your skin.

2. Why do people sweat?

_____

_____

_____

3. People who sweat need more liquid because _____

    a. it will give them more oxygen.

    b. they need more salt from the water.

    c. more water will help their blood pump better.

    d. they need to replace liquids lost through sweat.

responses	activity	skeleton	flexible
muscles	oxygen	liquid	evaporates

1. Choose the word from the word box above that best matches each definition. Write the word on the line below.

A. _____ some kind of action

B. _____ things that happen as a result of other actions

C. _____ when water breaks Into tiny drops and seems to disappear

D. _____ body parts that stretch and relax to help people move

E. _____ able to bend easily

F. _____ something that flows easily, like water

G. _____ one of the gases in the air that people need to live

H. _____ the frame of bones in the body

2. Fill in the blanks in the sentences below. Choose the word from the word box that completes each sentence.

A. The longer they ran, the more the runners gasped for

_____.

B. One of the body's _____ to exercise is to breathe faster.

C. Water, like oil, is a kind of _____.

D. She was so _____ that she could put her elbow behind her head.

E. Walking is a good _____ for people who want to become fit.

F. Everyone's _____ contains hundreds of bones.

G. Sweat cools the body as it _____.

H. After she ran for two hours, her leg _____ hurt from all the exercise.

Exercise and Your Body

1. Use the idea web to help you remember what you read. In each box, write the main idea of that reading.

What Happens to Your Body?

_____

_____

_____

_____

Exercise and the Skeleton

_____

_____

_____

_____

Exercise and Your Body

Exercise and Muscles

_____

_____

_____

Exercise and Skin

_____

_____

_____

2. What are two reasons people should exercise?

_____

_____

_____

_____

3. What are two ways your body responds to exercise?

_____

_____

_____

_____

4. What would you tell someone who wanted to learn about exercise and the body?

_____

_____

_____

_____

Earthquakes

A woman tries to save things from her home after an earthquake.

Fast Facts

- Most of the world's earthquakes take place in an area called the Ring of Fire.

- Most earthquakes last less than a minute.

- People may feel small movements in the ground even months after an earthquake.

What Is an Earthquake?

The walls of buildings start to shake. Pictures on the walls move back and forth. In some parts of the world, there are times[28] when people can feel the ground move. This movement is called an earthquake.[41]

We live on the Earth's crust. Earth's crust is broken into about seven large pieces and some smaller ones. These pieces[62] are called plates. The plates move, Earth shakes. Many times, these movements are too small for people to feel.[81]

When the movements are big, people can feel them. The ground moves and buildings may fall down. That movement is an earthquake.[103]

Earthquakes

A scientist tries to predict if an earthquake will happen.

Fast Facts

- Animals may hear sounds that warn them an earthquake is on the way.

- Waves from a major earthquake can be measured on the other side of the world.

- There is no way to prevent an earthquake from happening.

Predicting and Measuring Earthquakes

TV reports tell people when bad storms are coming. However, there's no report that tells when earthquakes are[22] on the way. Scientists can predict places where earthquakes could happen. They can't predict when an earthquake might[40] take place. Scientists keep looking for ways to predict earthquakes.[50]

After earthquakes happen, scientists measure their size. The ground's vibrations are measured on the nine points of the[68] Richter scale. When the vibrations measure 3.5 or higher on the Richter scale, people usually know that an earthquake has[88] happened. Earthquakes that measure 4.5 or higher on the Richter scale can harm buildings and roads.[104]

KEY NOTES

Predicting and Measuring Earthquakes

What is the Richter scale?

_____

_____

Earthquakes

Workers "duck, cover, and hold" under a table for safety during an earthquake drill.

Fast Facts

- In a 1989 earthquake, bricks and stones that fell off buildings hurt many people.

- In places where there are many earthquakes, people have drills so they know what to do.

- School children get under their desks in earthquake drills.

Duck, Cover, and Hold

The three rules of earthquake safety are DUCK, COVER, and HOLD.[15]

DUCK means get under a table or sit next to a wall without windows. This position helps keep glass from a broken window[38] from hitting you. If you're outside, get off sidewalks and stay away from buildings, trees, and power lines.[56]

Next, COVER yourself with a rug or coat. Or put your head in your lap, with your arms around your head.[77]

HOLD means stay where you are, even when you think the earthquake's over. The earthquake may seem to have stopped, but it can start up again.[103]

KEY NOTES

Duck, Cover, and Hold
How do the three rules of earthquake safety keep people safe?

_____

_____

Earthquakes

A tsunami just hit this area near the ocean.

Fast Facts

- A tsunami wave looks like a huge wall of water.

- Tsunamis pick up and suck in objects.

- A tsunami wave is strong enough to kill people and damage buildings.

Underwater Earthquakes

When earthquakes happen underwater, vibrations that move through the water cause waves to form. The waves get[19] bigger and faster as they move out from the earthquake's center. The waves can travel faster than 400 miles per hour.[40] That's about the same speed as an airplane. They can grow to 100 feet, about as high as a six-story building.[62]

In Japan, where many people live close to the water, the waves made by underwater earthquakes were given the name[82] *tsunami,* which means "harbor wave." These waves were given this name because tsunamis can harm the people and things around harbors.[103]

<table>
<tr><td colspan="2" align="center">KEY NOTES</td></tr>
<tr><td colspan="2">Underwater Earthquakes
What causes waves to form in a tsunami?

_____

_____</td></tr>
</table>

Earthquakes

What Is an Earthquake?

1. Another good name for "What Is an Earthquake?" is _____

    a. "Earth's Crust."
    b. "Why Buildings Fall Down."
    c. "The Shaking Earth."
    d. "The Earth Has Plates."

2. Why did the author write "What Is an Earthquake?"

    a. to give readers information about earthquakes
    b. to compare big earthquakes and small earthquakes
    c. to compare different kinds of plates
    d. to tell about his experience during an earthquake

3. What is an earthquake?

_____

_____

_____

Predicting and Measuring Earthquakes

1. In this reading, *predict* means _____

_____

_____

_____

2. This reading is MAINLY about _____

    a. why scientists cannot measure earthquakes.

    b. how earthquakes are reported on TV.

    c. how the Richter scale was invented.

    d. the fact that scientists cannot predict earthquakes, but they can measure them.

3. Explain your answer to question 2.

_____

_____

_____

Duck, Cover, and Hold

1. What is the main idea of "Duck, Cover, and Hold"?

    a. how to cover your head in an earthquake

    b. how to predict earthquakes

    c. how to know when an earthquake is over

    d. how to stay safe in an earthquake

2. If you are in an earthquake, what should you do FIRST?

_____

_____

_____

3. Why do you think it is important to have rules for earthquake safety?

_____

_____

_____

Underwater Earthquakes

1. In this reading, the word *vibrations* means _____

    a. waves that move quickly.
    b. a shaking movement.
    c. waves that grow high.
    d. things that live underwater.

2. What happens to the ocean in an underwater earthquake?

    a. The water moves around a little.
    b. Big, fast waves can form.
    c. Boats rock in the sea.
    d. People get on airplanes.

3. Why are tsunamis called harbor waves?

_____

_____

_____

| earthquake | harbor | Japan | predict |
| Richter | sidewalk | tsunami | vibrations |

1. Choose the word from the word box above that best matches each definition. Write the word on the line below.

A. _____ to say what is going to happen

B. _____ a country in Asia

C. _____ a shaking of the ground

D. _____ a walkway

E. _____ shaking or moving

F. _____ a scale to measure earthquakes

G. _____ a wave from an underwater earthquake

H. _____ a place for boats that is usually safe

2. Fill in the blanks in the sentences below. Choose the word from the word box that completes each sentence.

A. An _____ makes the ground move.

B. We could feel the _____ on the track as the train went by.

C. A big ship came into the _____.

D. The earthquake measured 6 on the _____ scale.

E. My teacher visited _____ last summer.

F. Sam rode his bike on the _____.

G. It is hard to _____ if our team will win.

H. The _____ made the ships rock in the sea.

Earthquakes

1. Use the idea web to help you remember what you read. In each box, write the main idea of that reading.

What Is an Earthquake?

_____

_____

_____

_____

Predicting and Measuring Earthquakes

_____

_____

_____

_____

Earthquakes

Duck, Cover, and Hold

_____

_____

_____

_____

Underwater Earthquakes

_____

_____

_____

_____

2. Write the most interesting thing you read about earthquakes. Explain your choice.

_____

_____

_____

_____

3. Write a question you would like to ask the author about earthquakes.

_____

_____

_____

_____

4. How would you explain earthquakes to someone who didn't know about them?

_____

_____

_____

_____

Inventions

Rebecca Schroeder uses the glow-in-the-dark clipboard that she invented to solve a problem.

Fast Facts

- The bicycle was invented in Europe and was first ridden in 1817.

- The first gas-powered car was used on the streets in 1886.

- A 10-year-old boy invented a glow-in-the-dark toilet seat.

What Is an Invention?

Today, we travel by car, watch television, and turn on lights. Not long ago, though, none of these things existed. Each one is an invention, and each has changed the world.[35]

Sometimes inventions are created when people try to solve a problem. When Rebecca Schroeder couldn't see to do her [54] homework in the car after dark, she invented a glow-in-the-dark clipboard. Today, nurses in hospitals use this invention. Late at[77] night, hospital nurses can see to write notes without waking sick people because Rebecca Schroeder had a problem she solved by inventing something.[100]

KEY NOTES

What Is an Invention?
What is one reason people invent things?

_____

_____

Inventions

Arthur Fry found a new use for a weak glue by inventing sticky notes.

Fast Facts

- Some bugs love to eat the glue on stamps.

- The oldest glue in the world is about 8,200 years old.

- People have made glue from fish, beeswax, flour, and egg whites.

Finding the Right Use

Sometimes researchers don't know they have invented something useful. A researcher named Spencer Silver created a[20] glue that was too weak to hold things together for a long time. Silver stopped working on the glue, but Arthur Fry thought he could use it.[47]

Fry often lost his place in his songbook at church, so he put the weak glue on little pieces of paper and stuck them to the[73] pages of his songbook. The little pieces of paper helped Fry find his place, and the weak glue didn't harm the songbook. That's how sticky notes were created.[101]

KEY NOTES

Finding the Right Use
What problem did Arthur Fry have?

_____

_____

Inventions

Today, the Kevlar® in helmets helps protect people.

Fast Facts

- Kevlar vests protect police officers from gunshots.

- Hundreds of millions of dollars of Kevlar products are sold every year.

- Space suits are made of Kevlar.

An Invention That Saves Lives

In 1964, an inventor was looking for a way to make car tires stronger. Nothing she tried worked well. Then, she made[27] something unlike any material anyone had made. This new material was five times stronger than steel. The material, which became known as Kevlar, made car tires stronger and safer.[56]

Kevlar can be used to save lives, too. It is used in helmets that people wear when they ride bikes, ski, or do other sports.[81] These helmets keep people safe when they fall and hit their head. The Kevlar in the helmet protects the head inside it.[103]

KEY NOTES

An Invention That Saves Lives
What is Kevlar?

_____

_____

Inventions

Calculators have changed since the first ones were invented.

Fast Facts

- An ancient kind of calculator, called an abacus, uses beads on a frame.

- The smallest calculator is only as big as ten molecules.

- Some of the first calculators weighed 55 pounds and cost $2,500.

An Invention That Keeps Changing

Some inventions, like calculators, keep getting better. Calculators are like adding machines. People use them to add numbers and to solve other kinds of math problems.[31]

At first, calculators were so huge they took up a whole room. The first calculators were also very expensive, and it took many people to use them.[58]

Today, all that has changed. Calculators are no longer expensive. People can buy them for a few dollars. They are[78] small, too. Some are smaller than a person's hand. These days, most people can buy and use calculators. Like many useful inventions, calculators keep getting better.[104]

KEY NOTES

An Invention That Keeps Changing
Why might an invention keep changing?

_____

_____

Inventions

What Is an Invention?

1. What is an invention?

    a. a person who invents something
    b. a problem that needs to be solved
    c. a company that makes new things
    d. a new thing or new way of doing something

2. What problem was solved with a glow-in-the-dark clipboard?

    a. getting well in a hospital
    b. driving a car in the dark
    c. seeing well enough to write in the dark
    d. taking notes in school

3. How could a problem lead to an invention?

_____

_____

_____

Finding the Right Use

1. The main idea of "Finding the Right Use" is _____

    a. anyone can be an inventor.
    b. all inventions can be useful in some way.
    c. a man named Fry invented a paper for songbooks.
    d. some inventions can be used in different ways.

2. Why did Spencer Silver stop working with glue?

_____

_____

_____

3. How did Arthur Fry use Spencer Silver's glue?

_____

_____

_____

An Invention That Saves Lives

1. Another good name for "An Invention That Saves Lives" is _____

    a. "How Kevlar Was Invented."
    b. "Women Inventors."
    c. "Helmets Save Lives."
    d. "Inventing Strong Tires."

2. Why was Kevlar invented?

_____

_____

_____

3. Kevlar is good for sports helmets because it _____

    a. is a very strong material.
    b. bends very easily.
    c. keeps in heat well.
    d. does not cost a lot.

An Invention That Keeps Changing

1. "An Invention That Keeps Changing" is MAINLY about _____

    a. who uses calculators today.
    b. how people use calculators.
    c. how calculators keep getting better.
    d. how to invent a way to solve math problems.

2. What are two ways calculators have changed?

_____

_____

_____

3. Describe an invention you know about that keeps changing.

_____

_____

_____

invention	hospital	researcher	create
Kevlar	helmet	calculator	expensive

1. Choose the word from the word box above that best matches each definition. Write the word on the line below.

A. _____ to make something new

B. _____ a tool that does math quickly

C. _____ a hat that keeps a person's head safe

D. _____ something that someone made that did not exist before

E. _____ a material that is very strong and is used to make tires

F. _____ costing a lot of money

G. _____ a place where doctors and nurses take care of the sick

H. _____ a person who studies things

2. Fill in the blanks in the sentences below. Choose the word from the word box that completes each sentence.

A. Because he wanted to stay safe, he wore a _____ when he went biking.

B. The _____ studied how medicines worked in people.

C. You might buy a shirt because it is less _____ than a similar one.

D. _____ is often used in space suits because it is so strong.

E. My friend broke her leg and had to go to the _____.

F. An artist might use paints to _____ a painting.

G. Because there were so many numbers to add, Bob used a _____.

H. Maria thinks the phone is the best _____ because it changed so many lives.

47

Inventions

1. Use the idea web to help you remember what you read. In each box, write the main idea of that reading.

What Is an Invention?

_____

_____

_____

_____

Finding the Right Use

_____

_____

_____

_____

Inventions

An Invention That Saves Lives

_____

_____

_____

_____

An Invention That Keeps Changing

_____

_____

_____

_____

2. How are all inventions alike?

_____

_____

_____

_____

3. Describe how two of the inventions you learned about in this topic
have made people's lives better.

_____

_____

_____

_____

4. What do you think is the most useful invention? Explain your choice.

_____

_____

_____

_____

Masks

Masks may be worn during important ceremonies.

Fast Facts

- Cave paintings from more than 10,000 years ago show people wearing masks.

- Ancient Greeks at war wore masks to scare people they were fighting.

- Some American Indian masks are carved from living trees.

Masks Through Time

For thousands of years, people around the world have used masks. Masks have often been used in important ceremonies.[22] For example, if ancient people did a dance to ask the gods to help a sick person, they might wear masks to honor forces that they believed could help the person get well.[55]

Today, in some ceremonies, people dance to tell stories. Wearing masks helps dancers play the parts of people in the stories and honor them.[79]

Some masks only cover a person's face, while others cover the head and shoulders. Masks have been made of animal skins,[100] wood, metal, and clay. Some masks are simple, while others take months to make.[114]

KEY NOTES

Masks Through Time
Why do some dancers wear masks?

_____

_____

Masks

King Tut's death mask is more than 3,000 years old.

Fast Facts

- King Tut's death mask weighs about 24 pounds.

- In Egyptian death masks, the eyes of kings are wide open.

- King Tut became king at the age of nine and died when he was in his teens.

Egyptian Death Masks

Many groups of people have made masks for their dead. Artists in ancient Egypt made death masks for their kings. After [24] the king died, the artist made a wax mold of the king's face. From the wax mold, the artist then made the mask. If a king was [51] very important, his mask might be covered with gold and gems. Ancient Egyptians believed that the king's death mask would help the king make his way to the afterlife. [80]

The most famous death mask from Egypt was made for King Tut more than 3,000 years ago. The smooth, golden face of the dead king is known to people around the world. [112]

KEY NOTES

Egyptian Death Masks

How were ancient Egyptian death masks made for kings?

_____

_____

Masks

This African mask is made from wood.

Fast Facts

- Some modern artists base their art on the masks of Africa.

- Rare African masks may sell for hundreds of thousands of dollars.

- Mask makers may study for years before they make a mask on their own.

African Masks

Masks have long been an important part of life in many parts of Africa. Some African people make spirit masks based on[24] powerful animals, such as hawks. These masks are used in ceremonies in which people honor these spirits and ask them[44] for help. Other people honor their ancestors by making masks of their faces and using the masks in dances. These dances ask the ancestors for their help.[71]

Among some people, the look of the masks has stayed the same for centuries, even though new masks have been made[92] through the years. Many people think that if the mask looks different, the spirit won't know it is being called.[112]

KEY NOTES

African Masks

Why might people make masks of powerful animals?

_____

_____

Masks

These actors are wearing masks like those of ancient Greece.

Fast Facts

- Ancient Greek masks were made so actors' voices carried far into the crowd.

- Only men were actors in Greece, so men wore masks to play women's roles.

- It took 750 pounds of rubber to make the masks for *The Lion King*.

Theater Masks

Masks have been used since theater began. Actors in the theaters of ancient Greece and Rome wore masks. The faces on[23] the masks showed the feelings of their character: sad, happy, or angry. Only men were actors, so to play a woman's part, men wore masks with women's faces.[51]

Today, masks are used in some kinds of theater. In some well-known shows, like *The Lion King,* many actors wear masks.[73] The show's main roles are played by actors who wear huge animal masks that make them look like lions, zebras, and other[95] animals. The masks allow the actors to look like animals even as they talk and act like human beings.[114]

KEY NOTES

Theater Masks

What did the theater masks of ancient Greece and Rome show?

_____

_____

Masks

Masks Through Time

1. Another good name for "Masks Through Time" is _____

    a. "Dancing and Masks."
    b. "Masks of Yesterday and Today."
    c. "Ancient Masks."
    d. "What Masks Are Made Of."

2. Some ancient people wore masks to _____

    a. ask the gods to help someone get well.
    b. help tell stories about ceremonies.
    c. teach children about history.
    d. scare other people.

3. What are two reasons a storyteller might wear a mask?

_____

_____

_____

Egyptian Death Masks

1. What is the main idea of "Egyptian Death Masks"?

    a. People of every country make death masks.
    b. King Tut is the most famous king of Egypt.
    c. Ancient Egyptians made mummies.
    d. Ancient Egyptians made death masks for kings.

2. How were ancient Egyptian death masks made?

_____

_____

_____

3. Why did the ancient Egyptians make death masks for their kings?

_____

_____

_____

African Masks

1. African masks are often used to _____

    a. ask spirits for help.
    b. show how rich a tribe is.
    c. make music.
    d. tell stories to children.

2. Why have many masks looked the same for centuries?

_____

_____

_____

3. How do some African people feel about their ancestors?

_____

_____

_____

Theater Masks

1. "Theater Masks" is MAINLY about _____

    a. masks that are used in *The Lion King*.
    b. animal masks worn in theaters.
    c. how to make theater masks.
    d. different kinds of theater masks.

2. In ancient Rome and Greece, masks in plays showed _____

    a. who was a singer.
    b. whether an actor was a man or a woman.
    c. what country actors came from.
    d. the characters' feelings.

3. Why might actors wear masks?

_____

_____

_____

ceremonies	spirit	Egypt	artist
honor	ancestors	theater	actors

1. Choose the word from the word box above that best matches each definition. Write the word on the line below.

A. _____ people who perform in plays or movies

B. _____ a country in North Africa

C. _____ a being that some people believe lives on after death

D. _____ people who were born before someone in a family

E. _____ to give special respect to

F. _____ a person who makes art

G. _____ a place where plays are shown

H. _____ a set of actions done in a special way

2. Fill in the blanks in the sentences below. Choose the word from the word box that completes each sentence.

A. Two new _____ played the roles of the two brothers in that play.

B. I watched the _____ paint a painting.

C. When he sang the song, he felt the _____ of his grandmother.

D. We _____ soldiers because they are brave.

E. My class went to the _____ to see a play.

F. I want to visit the country of _____ to see the mummies.

G. I have two _____ who came from Africa.

H. Often there are _____ when people marry.

Masks

1. Use the idea web to help you remember what you read. In each box, write the main idea of that reading.

Masks Through Time

_____

_____

_____

Egyptian Death Masks

_____

_____

_____

Masks

African Masks

_____

_____

_____

Theater Masks

_____

_____

_____

2. What are two ways masks were used in ancient times?

_____

_____

_____

_____

3. How might an actor play a part differently with a mask or without one?

_____

_____

_____

_____

4. What are two things you learned about masks in these readings?

_____

_____

_____

_____

Jazz

A jazz band plays together in the early 20th century.

Fast Facts

- At first, musicians used the word *jass* to mean what we now call jazz.

- Many people think the first real jazz music dates from around the beginning of the 20th century.

- The first jazz record was made in 1917.

Jazz Begins

Jazz was born in the United States more than a century ago. Nobody can say exactly when, because jazz grew slowly. When[24] Africans were brought to North America, they brought their music with them. They continued to play drums and sing using[44] African rhythms. When those rhythms met the simple tunes of people who had come from Europe, a new music was born. This music became known as jazz.[71]

In other places around the world, white and black people lived near each other but did not mix. It was only in the United[95] States, where slaves and owners lived near one another, that the bright rhythms and simple tunes blended into jazz.[114]

KEY NOTES

Jazz Begins

What are the two parts of music that blend to make jazz?

_____

_____

Jazz

This jazz band had many different instruments in it, including piano and horns.

Fast Facts

- There are hundreds of different kinds of drums in Africa.

- Horns are in the brass section of a jazz band because horns are made of brass, which is a mix of metals.

- Early jazz piano music was called ragtime.

Making Jazz

In Africa, drums have long been used to carry news from village to village. When African slaves arrived in North America,[23] they made drums from logs or kegs. Then, slave holders became afraid that drums could help slaves plan escapes, so slaves[44] weren't allowed to use drums. Instead, they clapped the beat of their songs.[57]

Later, European music was combined with African music. Pianos and horns combined with drums and made music with a[76] strong beat. Although both use the same instrument, jazz piano music and European piano music sound different. Jazz piano[95] music has a lively rhythm and a strong beat. Often, the music is created as the piano player plays.[114]

KEY NOTES

Making Jazz

How did African and European music combine to make jazz?

_____

_____

Jazz

Wynton Marsalis has played the trumpet since he was a child.

Fast Facts

- Wynton Marsalis was born in New Orleans, Louisiana, which is also the birthplace of jazz.

- Four of the six Marsalis brothers became musicians.

- Wynton Marsalis's records have sold about 5 million copies.

Wynton Marsalis

Wynton Marsalis grew up playing jazz. His father, a music teacher who played piano, and his mother, a singer, taught their[23] children to love music. As a child, Wynton Marsalis played the trumpet in a church marching band. As a teen, he toured the[46] world playing jazz. In 1982, Wynton Marsalis started a jazz band with one of his brothers. Their band toured the world.[67]

Today, Wynton Marsalis plays the trumpet and writes music. In 1997, he won an important award for music he wrote[87] about slavery. Marsalis also teaches music to young people. Through his teaching and his love of music, Wynton Marsalis has taught many young people to love jazz.[114]

KEY NOTES

Wynton Marsalis
Write a new title for this reading. Explain your choice.

_____

_____

Jazz

Jazz musicians experiment to create different sounds and types of jazz.

Fast Facts

- The 1920s were called the Jazz Age because it seemed everyone was playing jazz music.

- One kind of jazz dance was called the bunny hug.

- Scat singing in jazz uses only nonsense words.

Jazz Changes

Jazz has changed through the years because jazz musicians love to experiment. In the 1920s, some musicians mixed jazz[21] with classical music. They called this music "jazzing the classics."[31]

In the 1930s, large groups of musicians played a kind of jazz called Big Band, or swing, music. Starting in the late 1940s,[54] on the West Coast, the sound was called "cool jazz," and it was slower and sometimes based on classical music. On the East Coast, jazz musicians played a harder jazz sound.[85]

Today, experimenting continues. Jazz musicians enjoy bringing different musical sounds into the music they love. In[101] addition, the jazz beat has had an effect on other music, including hip-hop.[114]

KEY NOTES

Jazz Changes

How can people experiment with music?

_____

_____

Jazz

Jazz Begins

1. This passage is MAINLY about _____

    a. famous jazz players.
    b. jazz in Africa.
    c. how jazz started.
    d. who plays jazz.

2. How did the music of Africa and Europe combine to make jazz?

_____

_____

_____

3. Why did the music of black and white people mix more easily in the United States?

_____

_____

_____

Making Jazz

1. Why didn't slave holders allow slaves to have drums?

_____

_____

_____

2. Another good name for "Making Jazz" is _____

    a. "Piano and Drums."
    b. "The Instruments of Jazz."
    c. "Drums From Africa."
    d. "How to Make Drums."

3. How would you describe jazz music?

_____

_____

_____

Wynton Marsalis

1. The main idea of "Wynton Marsalis" is that Marsalis _____

    a. comes from a family of musicians.
    b. and his brother toured the world.
    c. writes jazz music.
    d. is a famous jazz musician.

2. What are two things Wynton Marsalis does as a jazz musician?

_____

_____

_____

3. Wynton Marsalis's family _____

    a. encouraged him to play music.
    b. all play in his band.
    c. all play trumpets.
    d. are well-known singers.

Jazz Changes

1. Jazz has changed through the years _____

    a. as musicians were paid more.
    b. when people began to dance to jazz.
    c. when jazz replaced rock music.
    d. because musicians experimented.

2. What are two ways classical and jazz music were mixed?

_____

_____

_____

3. Experimenting in jazz happens today when musicians _____

    a. bring different music into jazz.
    b. learn to play African music.
    c. play Big Band music.
    d. "jazz the classics."

| rhythm | jazz | combined | **Wynton Marsalis** |
| trumpet | musicians | piano | classical |

1. Choose the word from the word box above that best matches each definition. Write the word on the line below.

A. _____ people who make music

B. _____ mixed things together

C. _____ relating to a type of music that has been made for many years

D. _____ a large box with keys that a player presses to make music

E. _____ a metal horn that can be used to make music

F. _____ the pattern of beats in music

G. _____ a form of music that began in the United States

H. _____ a well-known jazz musician

2. Fill in the blanks in the sentences below. Choose the word from the word box that completes each sentence.

A. She counted out the beats in the _____ of the song.

B. The horn she played was a gold-colored _____.

C. The _____ piano piece was exciting.

D. _____ has helped get young people interested in jazz.

E. In the concert, the _____ played the songs we loved.

F. He combined European and _____ music with American jazz.

G. A _____ makes music when people play on the keys.

H. The song _____ two different kinds of music.

Jazz

1. Use the idea web to help you remember what you read. In each box, write the main idea of that reading.

Jazz Begins
_____
_____
_____
_____

Making Jazz
_____
_____
_____
_____

Jazz

Wynton Marsalis
_____
_____
_____
_____

Jazz Changes
_____
_____
_____
_____

2. Why is jazz thought to be mainly a U.S. music form?

_____

_____

_____

_____

3. What do you think makes jazz different from other kinds of music?

_____

_____

_____

_____

4. How do you think jazz is mixed with popular music today?

_____

_____

_____

_____

The poster was one way to advertise in the 19th century.

Fast Facts

- A poster of the movie *The Mummy* sold for nearly a half-million dollars.

- The longest advertising poster, for an opera in Rome, was nearly 899 feet long.

- The Library of Congress has the largest collection of posters in the world.

Early Posters

Long ago, people learned the news from a town crier, who shouted out important things that had happened. When the[22] printing press was invented in the 15th century, the news could spread much faster because presses could copy news items that[43] could be hung around the town. Then, the first posters appeared. Early posters usually included only the king's orders or advertised fairs or markets.[67]

By the 19th century, a new way of printing was invented, making it possible for artists to create brightly colored posters.[88] Posters with big pictures advertised everything from soap to plays. Today, it is common to see posters that advertise movies, bands, sports, and even countries.[113]

KEY NOTES

Early Posters

What did early posters show?

_____

_____

Posters

This poster came from the work of an artist in France.

Fast Facts

- The first famous poster artist, Jules Cheret, designed about 1,000 posters.

- The first American poster was designed for a circus in 1890.

- Many art museums make money by creating posters of their artists' work.

Posters as Art

Beginning in 1867, artists in France designed such beautiful posters that people began to think of posters as art. Some artists[24] used bold colors and bright figures to design posters for plays and singers. The work of these artists proved that even art used for advertising could be beautiful.[52]

Today, posters are still used to advertise products and events. However, it is also common to see posters used as[72] decoration. Many people decorate their living rooms, bedrooms, and offices with posters. These posters might show peoples'[89] favorite bands or movies, or the work of artists they like. Posters might also express ideas that people want others to think about.[112]

KEY NOTES

Posters as Art

How are posters used in advertising?

_____

_____

Posters

This popular poster was used to get people to go to war.

Fast Facts

- The artist who painted the poster of Uncle Sam used himself as a model.

- Before it became a poster, the painting of Uncle Sam was a magazine cover.

- Between 1917 and 1918, 4 million copies of the Uncle Sam poster were made.

"I Want You!"

Nearly 100 years ago, a poster appeared with an image of an old man who pointed his finger and said, "I want you for U.S. Army."[29]

The poster first appeared as the United States entered World War I. The image of the man, who became known as[50] Uncle Sam, stood for the United States. The popular image of his stern look and pointing finger caught people's attention. It also helped them decide to join the armed forces.[80]

The Uncle Sam poster was also used to get people to become soldiers in World War II. Even today, posters are a popular way to get people to join the armed forces.[112]

KEY NOTES

"I Want You!"
Why is the Uncle Sam poster important?

_____

_____

Posters

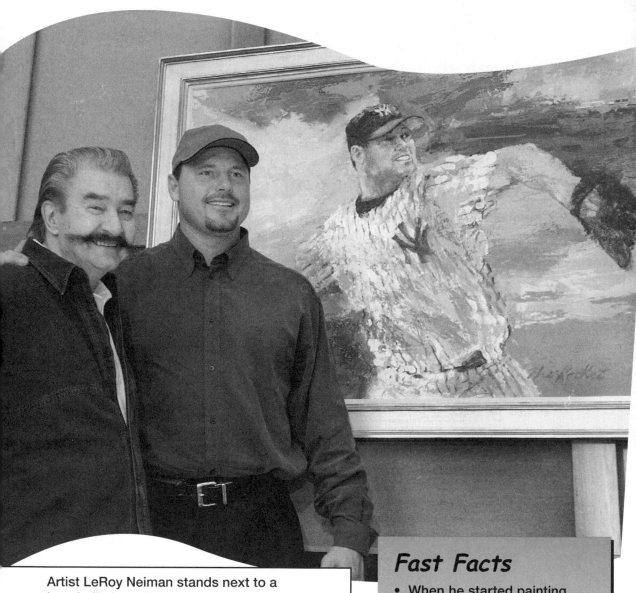

Artist LeRoy Neiman stands next to a baseball player that he painted.

Fast Facts

- When he started painting, LeRoy Neiman was so poor he painted with house paint.

- LeRoy Neiman painted 40-foot-high works of a dancer on a wall in New York City.

- LeRoy Neiman may be the richest artist in the United States.

A Poster Artist

LeRoy Neiman's paintings are colorful and full of energy, which may be why his fans love his images. His brightly colored[24] paintings have been made into posters that have sold thousands of copies.[36]

Although LeRoy Neiman grew up poor, he used his art to earn fame and money. In high school, Neiman was known for his posters of school dances and sports games.[66]

Later, Neiman developed a way of painting sports that made him very popular. His quick, colorful strokes catch the action of[87] a boxing match or a baseball game. People who love playing or watching sports can enjoy the power of the action in LeRoy Neiman's posters.[112]

KEY NOTES

A Poster Artist   Underline the sentence that tells how Neiman's work shows action. Explain your choice.

_____

_____

Posters

Early Posters

1. This passage is MAINLY about _____

    a. advertising.
    b. poster artists.
    c. who buys posters.
    d. how posters have changed.

2. Posters were first used to _____

    a. advertise things.
    b. sell movies.
    c. decorate walls.
    d. show pictures of the king.

3. How did the poster change in the 19th century?

_____

_____

_____

Posters as Art

1. Why did people begin to think of posters as art?

_____

_____

_____

2. The main idea of "Posters as Art" is that _____

    a. all posters are art.
    b. it is easy to make posters.
    c. French artists make beautiful posters.
    d. posters can be beautiful and used for decoration.

3. How are posters used today?

_____

_____

_____

"I Want You!"

1. Another good name for "I Want You!" is _____

    a. "Uncle Sam."
    b. "Posters and War."
    c. "Famous Posters."
    d. "Soldiers on Posters."

2. What was the "I Want You!" poster used for?

_____

_____

_____

3. In this reading, the word *image* means _____

    a. the Uncle Sam poster.
    b. how something looks.
    c. a beautiful poster.
    d. something that is seen by many people.

A Poster Artist

1. LeRoy Neiman is well known as _____

    a. a sports fan.
    b. a buyer of sports posters.
    c. an artist who paints sports.
    d. a sports star who makes posters.

2. Describe how LeRoy Neiman's paintings look.

_____

_____

_____

3. Sports fans like LeRoy Neiman's work because _____

    a. he is a sports fan.
    b. he paints sports fans.
    c. he plays sports himself.
    d. he catches the action in sports.

advertise	invented	designed	decorate
image	popular	LeRoy Neiman	

1. Choose the word from the word box above that best matches each definition. Write the word on the line below.

A. _____ to tell about a product

B. _____ to make something look better

C. _____ liked by many people

D. _____ a famous sports artist

E. _____ a picture of something

F. _____ made a plan using color and lines

G. _____ made something that had never been made before

2. Fill in the blanks in the sentences below. Choose a word from the word box to complete each sentence.

A. The new poster by the artist _____ was hung on the wall.

B. Marty _____ a new way to keep the car clean.

C. The _____ on the dollar bill is of a famous president.

D. She was in charge of the _____ for the book's cover.

E. Juan knew the posters would be perfect to _____ his bedroom walls.

F. Emily wanted to sell her car and decided to _____ it in the newspaper.

G. The baseball poster was _____ and it was sold right away.

Posters

1. Use the idea web to help you remember what you read. In each box, write the main idea of that reading.

Early Posters

_____

_____

_____

_____

Posters as Art

_____

_____

_____

_____

Posters

"I Want You!"

_____

_____

_____

_____

A Poster Artist

_____

_____

_____

_____

2. What are three ways people have used posters?

_____

_____

_____

_____

3. If you could put a poster on your wall, which of the posters you read about would you choose?

_____

_____

_____

_____

4. How have posters changed since they were first made?

_____

_____

_____

_____

Our National Government

The three branches of the U.S. government work together for the people.

Fast Facts

- More than 3 million people work for the U.S. government.

- Like the national government, U.S. state governments usually have three branches.

- The government of the Republic of China has five branches.

Who's in Charge of Our Government?

We think of the president as being the head of our country. However, the president works with other leaders to run the nation.[29]

In fact, the United States government has three branches. Onc branch includes people who are elected to make the laws.[49] Another branch includes people who make sure the country's laws are followed. The president, who is also elected, is part of[70] this branch. The third branch includes people who are on the courts. These people decide what the laws mean.[89]

On a baseball team, the pitcher and catcher have different jobs. Like pitchers and catchers, people in each branch of[109] government have different jobs, yet they work together to run our country.[121]

KEY NOTES
Who's in Charge of Our Government?
How does the U.S. president work with other leaders?
_____
_____

Our National Government

The White House is the home of the president of the United States.

Fast Facts

- The president can only serve two four-year terms.

- A father and son have both been elected president twice in U.S. history.

- President William Henry Harrison spent the shortest time in office. He died after serving one month as president.

Leading the Way

The president of the United States leads the executive branch of government. The president has several jobs, including[21] planning how the country might spend its money and trying to pass new laws. The executive branch is in charge of the armed[44] forces, such as the army, and it handles law enforcement as well. The enforcement section of the executive branch makes sure[65] people follow the country's laws. Also, the president and the executive branch work with the leaders of other countries.[84]

Many people do many different kinds of jobs for the executive branch. These jobs include caring for our national[103] parks, keeping track of taxes, working in other countries for our government, and making sure the laws are enforced.[122]

KEY NOTES

Leading the Way

What is the executive branch of the U.S. government?

_____

_____

Our National Government

Members of Congress pass laws for the nation.

Fast Facts

- Congress has the power to decide if the United States should go to war.

- Altogether, 535 people make the laws for the United States.

- Congressman John Dingell of Michigan served for more than 50 years in Congress.

Making the Laws

All countries need laws that everyone in the country must follow. In the United States, Congress makes the laws for the[24] nation. Congress is part of the nation's legislative branch of government.[35]

Congress has two sections, which are called houses. One house is made up of 100 people; two people are elected from[56] each of the 50 states. The other house has many more members. The number of people in that house is based on how many[80] people live in the state. States with many people have more members than do states with fewer people. People in both[101] houses of the legislative branch create, discuss, and pass laws, and all laws must be passed by both houses of Congress.[122]

KEY NOTES

Making the Laws
What are the houses of Congress?

_____

_____

Our National Government

Former Justice Sandra Day O'Connor was the first woman to serve on the U.S. Supreme Court.

Fast Facts

- The U.S. Supreme Court was founded in 1789.

- Every year, the Supreme Court hears only about 100 of the 7,000 cases that are brought to it.

- The judges of the Supreme Court wear black robes when they are in court.

Deciding What the Laws Mean

The job of the third branch of government, called the judicial branch, is to decide what the laws mean. The Supreme[26] Court is the highest court in the United States, or the head of the judicial branch. The nine judges who make up the Supreme[50] Court have the final word on the meaning of a law. They are the only leaders of our nation who are not elected by the people.[76]

The Supreme Court judges hear from people who have different ideas about the meaning of a law. Then, they decide[96] which meaning they think is right. Only five of the nine judges need to agree for the Supreme Court to decide what a law means.[121]

KEY NOTES

Deciding What the Laws Mean
What is the judicial branch of government?

_____

_____

Our National Government

Who's in Charge of Our Government?

1. "Who's in Charge of Our Government?" is MAINLY about _____

    a. how baseball teams work.
    b. the branches of a tree.
    c. the president of the United States.
    d. how the U.S. government is set up.

2. A pitcher and catcher are like the U.S. government in that they _____

    a. all work for the government.
    b. must make sure that everyone follows the rules.
    c. have different jobs, yet they work together to get things done.
    d. have the same job, and they work together to get things done.

3. Describe the three branches of the United States government.

_____

_____

_____

Leading the Way

1. Another good name for "Leading the Way" is _____

    a. "The Executive Branch."
    b. "The President Runs the Army."
    c. "The President Works Alone."
    d. "The Executive Branch Makes the Laws."

2. Describe two things the president does.

_____

_____

_____

3. What are two jobs that people do who work for the executive branch?

_____

_____

_____

Making the Laws

1. What does Congress do?

    a. Congress makes the nation's laws.
    b. Congress elects the nation's judges.
    c. Congress enforces the nation's laws.
    d. Congress runs the national government.

2. How are the two parts of Congress different?

_____

_____

_____

3. Every law must be _____

    a. written by the executive branch.
    b. passed by both houses of Congress.
    c. voted on by the people of the country.
    d. created by the president of the United States.

Deciding What the Laws Mean

1. The Supreme Court decides _____

    a. what the nation's laws should be.
    b. who should be elected to Congress.
    c. what the government should do.
    d. what the nation's laws mean.

2. How does the Supreme Court make decisions?

_____

_____

_____

3. The members of the Supreme Court are the only government leaders who _____

    a. are not elected by the people.
    b. are made up of five judges.
    c. are elected by the people.
    d. are in the judicial branch.

elect	pitcher	executive	enforcement
Congress	legislative	judicial	Supreme Court

1. Choose the word from the word box above that best matches each definition. Write the word on the line below.

A. _____ the highest court in the United States

B. _____ the branch of government that makes laws

C. _____ the branch of government that includes the president

D. _____ to choose someone by voting for him or her

E. _____ the lawmaking bodies of the U.S. government

F. _____ making sure laws are followed

G. _____ in baseball, the person who throws the ball to the batter

H. _____ the branch of government that tells what the laws mean

2. Fill in the blanks in the sentences below. Choose the word from the word box that completes each sentence.

A. The _____ branch of government makes laws.

B. People in law _____ make sure the laws are followed by everyone.

C. The two houses of _____ make the laws for the country.

D. The catcher threw the ball back to the _____.

E. Our country's _____ branch tells what the laws mean.

F. The _____ is the highest court in the United States.

G. The president is part of the _____ branch of government.

H. Next week, our team will _____ a new captain.

Our National Government

1. Fill in the Venn diagram with information about the three branches of government. In the center area, write how all three are alike. In the outer areas, write how each branch is different from the others.

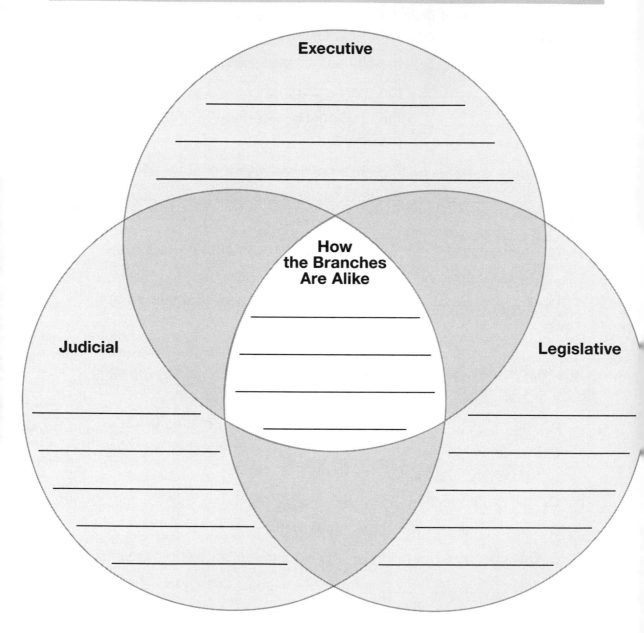

2. What jobs do people have in each branch of government?

_____

_____

_____

_____

3. Why do you think the government has three different branches?

_____

_____

_____

_____

4. What law would you like Congress to pass? Explain your answer.

_____

_____

_____

_____

Oceans

Most of Earth is covered by water.

Fast Facts

- Saltwater in the oceans makes up about 97 percent of Earth's water.

- Most ocean water is only 7°F above freezing.

- If the salt in the ocean were dried, it would cover all the continents 5 feet deep.

The Ocean

If you were in space looking at Earth, you would see more water than land. Water covers almost 75 percent of Earth. Most [25] of this water is in four oceans that are joined together. The oceans are really one big mass of water. Water is not all the same, [51] though. It has a variety of areas, from coasts to reefs to the ocean floor. [66]

The seven large land masses that rise above the oceans are called continents. Land masses that are smaller than continents [86] are called islands. Earth has many islands. While oceans and land masses are different in many ways, they are alike in one [108] important way. Beneath all of them—oceans, islands, and continents—is a layer of rock. [123]

KEY NOTES

The Ocean
What are the continents?

_____

_____

Oceans

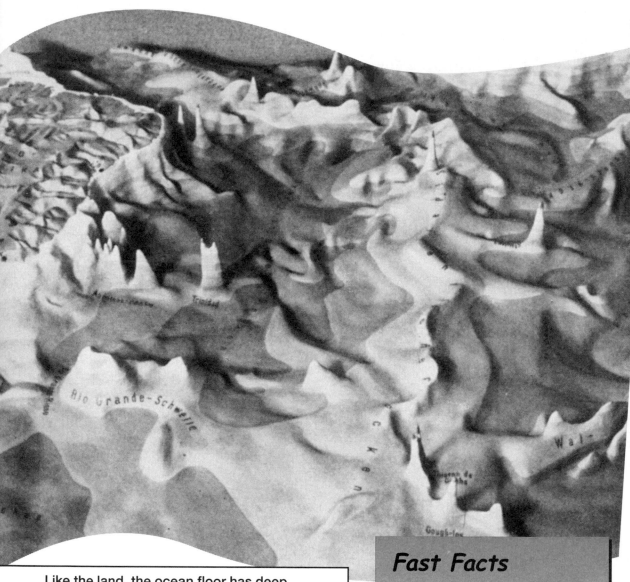

Like the land, the ocean floor has deep valleys, as shown in this underwater map.

Fast Facts

- The deepest part of the ocean is about 7 miles below the land.

- The largest waterfall on Earth, which is under the ocean, drops 2.2 miles.

- In the deepest part of the ocean, the pressure is as great as if one person tried to hold up 50 jets.

The Ocean Floor

On maps, the ocean floor looks smooth, but that's far from the truth. After new tools were invented, scientists discovered[23] that the ocean floor is like the land, with high mountains, deep valleys, and wide plains. In fact, the tallest mountain on Earth is[47] on the ocean floor. Maps now show this hidden world, with mountains, valleys, and plains that look like those that can easily be seen on land.[73]

At a continent's edge, the land slopes into the ocean. This slope of land is called the continental shelf. The ocean is not[96] very deep along the continental shelf. However, the continental shelf ends in a steep cliff. At the edge of this cliff, the ocean is very deep.[122]

KEY NOTES

The Ocean Floor
What happens to the land at the end of the continental shelf?

_____

_____

Oceans

Many kinds of plants and animals live on coral reefs.

Fast Facts

- Reefs can grow as slowly as one foot every 1,000 years.

- About 3,000 different species of marine life can live in a reef.

- Some reefs are more than 2 million years old.

Coral Reefs

The ocean has many layers, with different species of animals and plants in each one. In some warm places, the top[23] layer of the ocean is the habitat of little animals called corals. Each coral is about the size of a pen's tip.[45]

Corals live side by side and do not move. When corals die, their hard shells stick together. Then, new corals grow on top of[69] the old shells. Over a long time, piles of coral shells can grow very high, forming a coral reef.[88]

Some coral reefs look like large bushes. These reefs make good habitats for many animal and plant species because they[108] have lots of hiding places. People enjoy visiting coral reefs to see these underwater zoos.[123]

KEY NOTES

Coral Reefs
What is a coral reef?

_____

_____

Oceans

Over many years, ocean waves create sand by breaking stones into tiny pieces.

Fast Facts

- In the eastern United States, the coast is slowly sinking because the ocean level is rising.

- Weather and waves constantly change the shape of coasts.

- Coasts are rocky until the ocean has enough time to turn the rocks into sand.

Coasts

The winds that blow over the oceans make waves that move constantly. When the waves reach the land, they crash into an area of land called a coast.[29]

In some places, the land on the coast is made up of high cliffs. However, if the land on the coast is low, the constant[54] pounding of the waves can wear the land away, forming small rocks. The waves keep pounding these small rocks, breaking them into even smaller rocks.[79]

Over a very long time, the constant pounding of the waves breaks apart the small rocks, making them into tiny rock[100] particles. These particles finally become a wide sandy beach that people can visit to enjoy the sun and ocean waves.[120]

KEY NOTES

Coasts
What is a coast?

_____

_____

Oceans

The Ocean

1. Another good name for "The Ocean" is _____

    a. "Oceans in Space."
    b. "The Continents."
    c. "The Water on Earth."
    d. "Land Masses."

2. Describe how Earth looks from space.

_____

_____

_____

3. Most of the water on Earth is _____

    a. on the continents.
    b. in four oceans.
    c. on the coasts and the reefs.
    d. below Earth's surface.

The Ocean Floor

1. The main idea of "The Ocean Floor" is that _____

    a. the ocean floor is smooth like the water.
    b. the ocean floor has high and low areas, like the land.
    c. the ocean floor is always changing.
    d. there are few maps of the ocean floor.

2. Describe how the ocean floor looks.

_____

_____

_____

3. What is the continental shelf?

_____

_____

_____

Coral Reefs

1. A coral reef is made of _____

    a. several ocean layers.
    b. a pile of coral shells.
    c. a small ocean animal.
    d. piles of large bushes.

2. Where do corals live?

    a. in the top layer of the ocean
    b. on sea plants
    c. in the deep part of the ocean
    d. floating in the ocean

3. How do coral reefs form?

_____

_____

_____

Coasts

1. Which of the following is a fact about coasts?

    a. Waves slow down near the coasts.
    b. People have to build beaches to make coasts.
    c. Coasts are where ocean waves hit the land.
    d. Coasts are windy places.

2. What happens to waves when they reach the land?

_____

_____

_____

3. Why are some coasts sandy?

_____

_____

_____

habitat	species	valley	continents
islands	constant	particles	

1. Choose the word from the word box above that best matches each definition. Write the word on the line below.

A. _____ the seven large land masses on Earth

B. _____ very small pieces of something

C. _____ a group of plants or animals that are alike in some way

D. _____ the place where a kind of plant or animal is normally found

E. _____ without stopping

F. _____ a low area of land that lies between hills or mountains

G. _____ small land masses that have water around them

2. Fill in the blanks in the sentences below. Choose the word from the word box that completes each sentence.

A. Jason rode his bike up the mountain and then down into the _____.

B. One _____ of African dog doesn't bark.

C. That fish's _____ is in the coral reef, where there are lots of places to hide.

D. After many years, the _____ pounding of the waves created a sandy beach.

E. North and South America are two of the seven _____ on Earth.

F. There were many tiny _____ of sand on the beach.

G. Martin visited a small group of _____ with white, sandy beaches.

Oceans

1. Use the idea web to help you remember what you read. In each box, write the main idea of that reading.

The Ocean

_____

_____

_____

_____

The Ocean Floor

_____

_____

_____

_____

Oceans

Coral Reefs

_____

_____

_____

_____

Coasts

_____

_____

_____

_____

2. What are two facts you learned about the oceans in these readings?

_____

_____

_____

_____

3. How is the land under the oceans and on the continents alike?

_____

_____

_____

_____

4. Suppose there were another reading in this topic. Would you expect it to be about fish or about mountains? Why?

_____

_____

_____

_____

Ancient Egypt

This ancient Egyptian painting shows sailors on the Nile River.

Fast Facts

- In ancient Egypt, both men and women wore make-up.

- Many families in ancient Egypt had pet cats, perhaps because they helped to catch mice.

- People from countries who lost wars with ancient Egypt sometimes became slaves.

Egypt in Ancient Times

The Nile River runs through the country of Egypt. Until about 200 years ago, the Nile River flooded every year. This[25] same flooding occurred for thousands of years. The floods left rich soil on the land for six miles on each side of the river. This soil was good for growing crops.[56]

The river also helped Egypt's people travel from one place to another. People could easily buy and sell things by moving[77] them on the river. The good crops and easy travel helped make Egypt a rich country.[93]

Today, there still is a country of Egypt. When we talk about the things that occurred in Egypt thousands of years ago, though, we call it ancient Egypt.[121]

KEY NOTES

Egypt in Ancient Times
What was Egypt like in ancient times?

_____

_____

Ancient Egypt

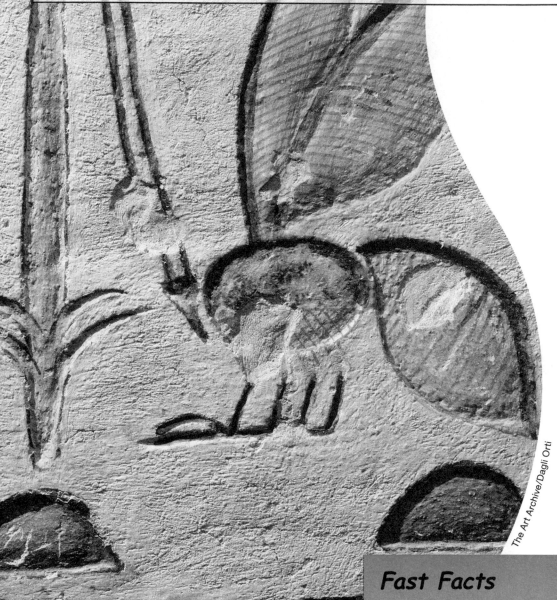

The Art Archive/Dagli Orti

This hieroglyph, which was carved into a king's tomb, says "King of Upper and Lower Egypt."

Fast Facts

- Fewer than 1 percent of ancient Egyptians could read or write.

- Egyptians wrote on paper made of pounded reeds, a kind of plant.

- Hieroglyphics could be written from left to right, from top to bottom, or from right to left.

Writing in Ancient Egypt

All of the words in English use the same 26 letters. These letters make up the English alphabet. The letters in the alphabet help us sound words out.[32]

Before people used an alphabet, they wrote with pictures and signs. The system of pictures ancient Egyptians used is[51] called hieroglyphics. Every word had its own picture or sign. Learning hieroglyphics was difficult. Those who could write had[70] honored jobs as scribes, but becoming a scribe meant going to school for twelve years.[85]

People in Egypt today no longer use hieroglyphics. Instead, they use an alphabet, as we do in English. Alphabets make[105] writing and reading easier because they allow people to make many words from a few letters.[121]

KEY NOTES

Writing in Ancient Egypt

Why was it difficult to learn to write with hieroglyphics?

_____

_____

Ancient Egypt

This museum shows how a room might have looked where mummies were made.

Fast Facts

- Cats and birds were also made into mummies.

- The ancient Egyptians believed in life after death, so they buried food that they thought the mummies might need.

- Workers might be killed and buried with a king so they could serve him after death.

124

Mummies

After ancient Egyptian kings and queens died, their bodies were made into mummies. When many people think of ancient Egypt, they think of these mummies.[26]

The process of making a mummy began right after death. First, priests took out most of the body's internal organs. The[47] brain, liver, and lungs were placed in stone jars. However, one internal organ, the heart, was usually left inside the body.[68] Priests then placed special plants on the body and wrapped it with strips of cloth.[83]

In modern times, people discovered several mummies and removed the strips of cloth. Because of the process the ancient[102] Egyptians used and the dry climate of Egypt, the mummies looked much like the bodies had looked right after the people died.[124]

KEY NOTES

Mummies
What new thing about mummies did you find out?

_____

_____

Ancient Egypt

The four sloping sides of a pyramid had to be built carefully so they could form a point.

Fast Facts

- The Great Pyramid covers 13 acres and was 481 feet tall when it was built.

- The pyramids were built so well that it is hard to slip paper between the blocks.

- No one is sure, but many think ramps were used to move the huge stone blocks.

The Pyramids

The mummies of kings and queens were kept in special
buildings called pyramids. A pyramid has four slanting sides[21]
that meet in a point at the top. The biggest pyramid, called the
Great Pyramid, was built by a king to be his home after death.[47]

There are more than 2 million stone blocks in the Great
Pyramid. To get an idea of the size of the Great Pyramid, picture[71]
a refrigerator. Each of the 2 million blocks in the Great Pyramid
is as heavy as 25 refrigerators.[89]

The workers had to put these heavy stone blocks in just
the right place. If the workers made a mistake and misplaced a
stone block, the four slanting sides wouldn't meet at the top.[123]

KEY NOTES

The Pyramids
What is a pyramid?

_____

_____

Ancient Egypt

Egypt in Ancient Times

1. Another good name for "Egypt in Ancient Times" is _____

    a. "Farming in Egypt."
    b. "Egypt and the Nile River."
    c. "Egypt Today."
    d. "Traveling in Egypt."

2. What happened to the soil near the river when the Nile River flooded?

_____

_____

_____

3. Why was ancient Egypt rich?

_____

_____

_____

Writing in Ancient Egypt

1. The main idea of "Writing in Ancient Egypt" is that _____

    a. people in Egypt today use hieroglyphics.
    b. people in ancient Egypt wrote using signs and pictures.
    c. signs and pictures make up an alphabet.
    d. people in ancient Egypt created the first alphabet.

2. What are hieroglyphics?

_____

_____

_____

3. Today, most Egyptians write with _____

    a. hieroglyphics.
    b. both hieroglyphics and an alphabet.
    c. language that has an alphabet.
    d. signs and pictures.

Mummies

1. Why did the ancient Egyptians make mummies?

    a. to save the bodies of everyone
    b. to keep people alive
    c. to make art
    d. to save the bodies of kings and queens

2. When they were discovered in modern times, the mummies looked _____

    a. like Egyptian kings and queens today.
    b. like the cloth had dried out their bodies.
    c. like they had right after they had died.
    d. like they were priests from ancient Egypt.

3. What were the steps of making a mummy in ancient Egypt?

_____

_____

_____

The Pyramids

1. "The Pyramids" is "MAINLY about _____

    a. how the Great Pyramid looks and how it was built.

    b. how kings and queens were buried.

    c. how to visit the Great Pyramid today.

    d. how long the Great Pyramid has lasted.

2. Describe the Great Pyramid.

_____

_____

_____

3. What two facts in the reading tell you how large the Great
    Pyramid is?

_____

_____

_____

Egypt	occurred	alphabet	hieroglyphics
internal	priest	pyramid	refrigerator

1. Choose the word from the word box above that best matches each definition. Write the word on the line below.

A. _____ someone who can perform religious services

B. _____ a stone building with four slanting sides that meet in a point at the top

C. _____ pictures or symbols that stand for words

D. _____ inside something else

E. _____ the letters of a language

F. _____ a box in which food is kept cold

G. _____ happened; took place

H. _____ a country in northeastern Africa

2. Fill in the blanks in the sentences below. Choose the word from the word box that completes each sentence.

A. The lungs and stomach are called _____ organs because they are inside the body.

B. Many homes were damaged when the storm _____.

C. When we write, we use an _____ that has 26 letters.

D. _____ is a hot, dry country in northern Africa.

E. Put the milk back in the _____ so it will stay cold.

F. In ancient Egypt, people used _____ to write, not letters.

G. A _____ was built for an important king in ancient Egypt.

H. A _____ usually marries people in a church.

Ancient Egypt

1. Use the idea web to help you remember what you read. In each box, write the main idea of that reading.

Egypt in Ancient Times

_____
_____
_____
_____

Writing in Ancient Egypt

_____
_____
_____
_____

Ancient Egypt

Mummies

_____
_____
_____
_____

The Pyramids

_____
_____
_____
_____

2. How was life in ancient Egypt different from life today?

_____

_____

_____

_____

3. How might having easy ways to travel help a country become rich?

_____

_____

_____

_____

4. Suppose there were another reading in this topic. Do you think it would be about modern Egypt or about how people lived in ancient Egypt? Explain your choice.

_____

_____

_____

_____

Adventure Writing

In adventure writing, people must often find a way to get themselves out of danger.

Fast Facts

- In a book called *Adrift*, the writer stayed alive on a raft in the ocean for 76 days.

- In 1996, after 12 people died climbing Mount Everest, at least 10 people wrote books about the climb.

- *Jaws,* an adventure story about sharks, has sold more than 10 million copies.

What Is Adventure Writing?

The hero hangs from a tree above a roaring river as a mountain lion swipes at him with a huge paw. Will the hero fall[29] into the river far below? We keep reading to find out. This is adventure writing at its best, writing that keeps readers[51] wondering what will happen next. It keeps readers turning the pages. In adventure writing, people often face problems that make it hard for them to stay alive.[78]

Sometimes adventure stories are true. They tell about things that really happened. Other stories are created by a writer. In[98] both kinds of adventure writing, people try to overcome dangers or problems.[110]

Many people like to read adventure writing because it's exciting. Perhaps they imagine themselves as the hero who can overcome any danger.[132]

KEY NOTES

What Is Adventure Writing?
Why do people like to read adventure stories?

_____

_____

Adventure Writing

This cover from an early printing of *The Call of the Wild* shows Buck leaping into the air.

Fast Facts

- *The Call of the Wild* has been translated into 68 languages.

- At least seven movies have been made of *The Call of the Wild*.

- The first printing of the book, 10,000 copies, sold out in one day.

The Call of the Wild

The Call of the Wild, by Jack London, is an adventure story in which the hero is a dog named Buck. In the story, Buck is stolen,[32] taken to Alaska, and treated badly. Then, Buck is saved by a man who treats him well, and he learns how to live in the cold Alaskan winter. Finally, Buck becomes the leader of a wild wolf pack.[70]

Although London wrote *The Call of the Wild* more than 100 years ago, readers around the world still love the story. At[92] first, they feel sorry for Buck. As the story goes on, though, they see him solve problems and make a home for himself. Finally,[116] readers see Buck living wild and free. Even though he is a dog, Buck is an adventure hero.[134]

KEY NOTES

The Call of the Wild

Why is Buck an adventure hero?

_____

_____

Adventure Writing

Jack London used his own travel experiences as he wrote many adventure stories and books.

Fast Facts

- Every day, Jack London wrote 1,000 words.

- London wrote more than 50 novels and dozens of short stories.

- Many of London's stories are about a person or animal returning to "the wild."

Jack London

Jack London, who wrote *The Call of the Wild,* led a life that was itself an adventure. He grew up poor and did different jobs all around the United States.[32]

Then, London went to Alaska, hoping to get rich during the gold rush. Instead, he found a frozen land where living was harsh. When London didn't find gold, he returned home.[63]

London could have been a postal worker, but he wanted a career as a writer. In 1899, the first story he sold was printed in[88] a magazine. London wrote many nature stories that were printed in magazines. He also wrote novels. He based much of[108] his work on his experiences in Alaska. Like an adventure hero, London had to solve many problems before he found a successful career as a writer.[134]

KEY NOTES

Jack London
Write a new title for this reading. Explain your choice.

_____

_____

Adventure Writing

This painting shows a ship drifting in the sea near the South Pole as the ice forms around it.

Fast Facts

- On a trip to the South Pole, a crew lived by eating seal and penguin meat.

- One book about climbing Mount Everest, written by a doctor, tells about saving lives at the top of the world.

- Steve Callahan, who drifted on a raft at sea, faced shark attacks and deep thirst.

True Adventures

Many people have written adventure stories. They have entertained their readers with fantastic stories of trips around the world, into the wild, and under the sea.[28]

Others have written about exciting and true adventures. Some have written about climbing the world's highest mountain.[45] Others have written about trying to sail to the South Pole, being trapped by ice, and nearly starving to death. One man wrote[68] about being lost at sea on a raft for 76 days. These stories can be even more exciting because the reader knows that they really happened.[94]

Whether or not they are true, readers find adventure stories entertaining. They think about what they might do if they[114] experienced these fantastic adventures. They also wonder if they would be as brave as the people they read about.[133]

KEY NOTES

True Adventures

What does the word *fantastic* mean in this reading?

_____

_____

Adventure Writing

What Is Adventure Writing?

1. This reading is MAINLY about _____

    a. what adventure writing is.
    b. why adventure writing always tells true stories.
    c. how to write an adventure story.
    d. famous people who write adventure stories.

2. Is adventure writing always true? Explain your answer.

_____

_____

_____

3. What are two reasons people read adventure writing?

_____

_____

_____

The Call of the Wild

1. Who is Buck?

    a. a man who saves a dog
    b. a dog
    c. a wolf
    d. a man who steals a dog

2. Another good name for *The Call of the Wild* is _____

    a. "A Hero Named Buck."
    b. "Dog Training in Alaska."
    c. "Wolves in the Wild."
    d. "Visiting Wild Alaska."

3. Describe what happens in *The Call of the Wild*.

_____

_____

_____

Jack London

1. Which of the following is a fact about Jack London?

    a. He wrote nature stories.
    b. He went to Alaska in the gold rush.
    c. He didn't find gold in Alaska.
    d. all of the above

2. Describe Jack London's life in Alaska.

_____

_____

_____

3. How was Jack London's life like an adventure story?

_____

_____

_____

True Adventures

1. Another good name for "True Adventures" is _____

    a. "Adventure Stories From Around the World."
    b. "Climbing Mountains."
    c. "Exciting Stories True and Invented."
    d. "Lost at Sea."

2. The main idea of this reading is that _____

    a. people love to read entertaining stories.
    b. people enjoy reading both real and fantastic stories.
    c. real adventure stories are more exciting than fantastic ones.
    d. people around the world write about their adventures.

3. How are true and fantastic adventures different?

_____

_____

_____

adventure	hero	Alaska	career
fantastic	magazine	entertain	

1. Choose the word from the word box above that best matches each definition. Write the word on the line below.

A. _____ the state that is farthest north in the United States

B. _____ to give others something to enjoy

C. _____ a job that someone wants to do for a while

D. _____ an exciting trip or experience

E. _____ a brave and strong person

F. _____ material that is printed regularly, such as every week or month

G. _____ very strange or not possible

2. Fill in the blanks in the sentences below. Choose the word from the word box that completes each sentence.

A. The _____ comes every month with new stories about life in the wilderness.

B. He loved to be in danger, and he wrote _____ tales about things he did.

C. They went to _____ in the winter to watch the sled dog races.

D. The _____ in the book bravely fought the lion.

E. The pop star sang to _____ her fans.

F. She liked to create stories, so she chose a _____ as a writer.

G. Some _____ stories have huge animals and trees that talk.

Adventure Writing

1. Use the idea web to help you remember what you read. In each box, write the main idea of that reading.

What Is Adventure Writing?

_____

_____

_____

The Call of the Wild

_____

_____

_____

Adventure Writing

Jack London

_____

_____

_____

True Adventures

_____

_____

_____

2. Why is *The Call of the Wild* an adventure book?

_____

_____

_____

_____

3. How did Jack London use his own experiences in his writing?

_____

_____

_____

_____

4. If you wrote an adventure story, what would it be about and where would it be set?

_____

_____

_____

_____

Many Ways to Communicate

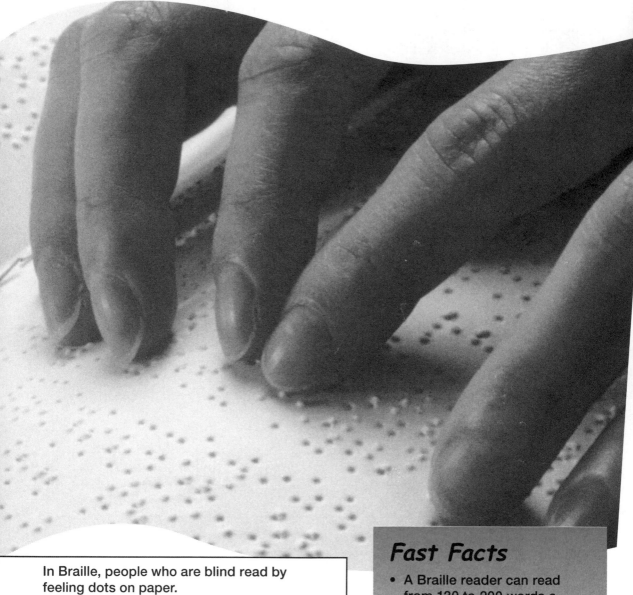

In Braille, people who are blind read by feeling dots on paper.

Fast Facts

- A Braille reader can read from 130 to 200 words a minute, or about the same rate that most people speak.

- The fastest Braille readers use both hands.

- There are football trading cards in Braille.

The Braille System

People can communicate in many different ways, sometimes without speaking. Today, people who can't see can communicate[20] by using a system called Braille. This system for reading and writing was developed by Louis Braille, a 15-year-old boy who was blind.[45]

Braille, who was born in 1809, knew about an army code for communicating at night. Each letter in the code used a pattern of raised dots. People read the dots with their fingertips.[78]

The army's system had as many as 12 dots for each letter. Braille made the code simpler, creating a six-dot system.[100] Although Louis Braille's system was easy to use, it took many years for people to understand its value. Today, blind people around the world read and write using the Braille system.[131]

KEY NOTES

The Braille System
What is the Braille system?

_____

_____

Many Ways to Communicate

During World War II, Germany used this machine to create a code that was very hard for its enemies to break.

Fast Facts

- Germany thought the code could never be broken and kept using it even after it had been solved.

- The 2001 movie *Enigma* tells how the code was broken.

- German code machines from World War II have sold for $20,000.

Germany's Secret Code

During World War II, Germany's armed forces used secret codes to communicate without words. These codes were made[21] and sent on special machines. Information about where to find English and U.S. ships was put into code so that German ships[43] could attack them. The secret code was based on only 26 letters, but it was very hard to break.[62]

For years, code breakers tried to figure out Germany's secret code. At one time, 1,000 people were trying to crack the code.[84] Finally, an English person figured out how the code worked. Then, English and U.S. forces could read the code and learn[105] about Germany's plans. They could also keep their ships out of danger. Breaking Germany's secret code helped England and the United States win the war.[130]

KEY NOTES

Germany's Secret Code   Why was Germany's secret code a problem for the English and U.S. forces?

_____

_____

Many Ways to Communicate

People who are deaf can choose to communicate by using American Sign Language.

Fast Facts

- ASL is the fourth most common language in the United States.

- Many Americans who are deaf think of ASL as their first language.

- ASL is different from British Sign Language, even though people in both countries speak English.

American Sign Language

American Sign Language, or ASL, is a language in which people use gestures, or movements, instead of words. Today,[22] many of the deaf people in North America use ASL to communicate with other people.[36]

ASL has its own words, word order, and rules. Although people gesture with their hands, they also use their eyes, lips,[57] and mouths to communicate with one another. For example, if people gesture with their hands about being angry, they also have an angry look on their face.[84]

Today's ASL grew out of American Indian sign languages as well as the work of some French teachers of deaf students.[105] As with other languages, American Sign Language continues to grow. New words are added in ASL just as they are in any other language to describe new ideas.[133]

KEY NOTES

American Sign Language
What is American Sign Language?

_____

_____

Many Ways to Communicate

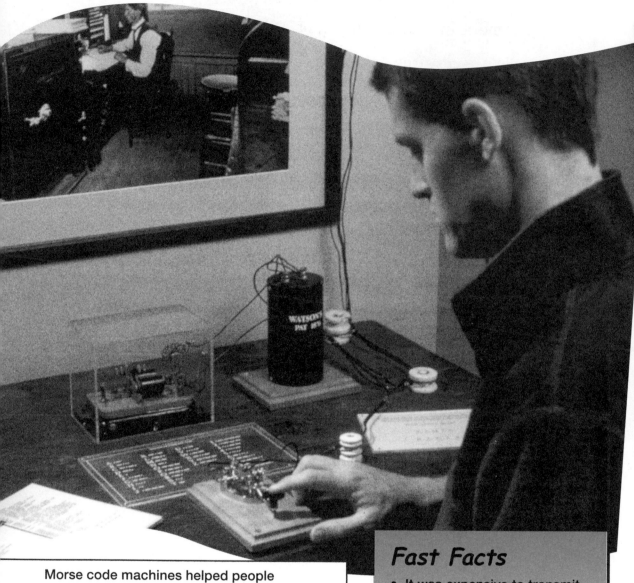

Morse code machines helped people communicate over long distances by sending a code over an electric wire.

Fast Facts

- It was expensive to transmit Morse code, so people used a few letters to represent whole words.

- Morse code experts have beat text message users in speed contests.

- The code for trouble, SOS, is easy to read—three dots, three dashes, three dots.

Morse Code

Samuel Morse was an American artist who also invented a special machine. This machine, which he invented in the 1830s,[22] sent information over an electric wire. Because wires could only carry short beats of sound, information was transmitted in code.[42] In Samuel Morse's code, short dots and longer dashes represented letters and numbers. For example, the letter *A* is[61] represented by a dot, then a dash. Morse code, as it became known, let people communicate without speaking.[79]

Morse code was used to transmit information across the United States. In 1866, an electric wire was placed under the[99] ocean that linked Europe and North America. By 1900, most of the world had Morse lines. Today, some ships and radio workers[121] still use the dots and dashes of Morse code to communicate without words.[134]

KEY NOTES

Morse Code
What is Morse code?

_____

_____

Many Ways to Communicate

The Braille System

1. Another good name for "The Braille System" is _____

    a. "Life in the 1800s."
    b. "Louis Braille's Life Story."
    c. "All About Blindness."
    d. "Communicating for People Who Are Blind."

2. Why did the author write "The Braille System"?

    a. to tell what it is like to be blind
    b. to tell readers how to use the Braille system
    c. to explain how the Braille system was created
    d. to tell how the army communicates at night

3. What are two facts about Braille?

_____

_____

_____

Germany's Secret Code

1. Name two facts you learned in "Germany's Secret Code."

_____

_____

_____

2. This reading is MAINLY about _____

    a. World War II.
    b. how code machines work.
    c. how breaking a code helped in war.
    d. when the German ships attacked English and U.S. ships.

3. Explain your answer to question 2.

_____

_____

_____

American Sign Language

1. In this reading, *gesture* means _____

    a. a movement someone makes.
    b. a language used by deaf people.
    c. an angry look.
    d. a way to make special sounds.

2. Another good name for "American Sign Language" is _____

    a. "A Special Language."
    b. "Communication."
    c. "How to Gesture."
    d. "New Words."

3. How is American Sign Language different from the spoken language that hearing people use?

_____

_____

_____

Morse Code

1. How does Morse code work?

_____

_____

_____

2. This reading is MAINLY about _____

   a. how to write messages in Morse code.
   b. how Morse code was created and used.
   c. communicating with sound.
   d. the life of Samuel Morse.

3. Explain your answer to question 2.

_____

_____

_____

communicate	secret	deaf	transmit
gesture	Germany	represent	

1. Choose the word from the word box above that best matches each definition. Write the word on the line below.

A. _____ a country that fought in World War II

B. _____ not able to hear

C. _____ to send

D. _____ a movement a person makes that gives information

E. _____ to share information with others

F. _____ something that is not known by others

G. _____ stand for, take the place of something

2. Fill in the blanks in the sentences below. Choose the word from the word box that completes each sentence.

A. The person who was _____ used ASL to tell the story.

B. To _____ with people in Mexico, I learned their language.

C. _____ created a secret code that was hard to break.

D. Sara's _____ showed us how to get to the gym.

E. The dots and dashes in Morse code _____ the ship's information.

F. Our _____ code helped our team signal to each other.

G. A cell phone can _____ messages around the world.

Many Ways to Communicate

1. Use the idea web to help you remember what you read. In each box, write the main idea of that reading.

The Braille System

_____

_____

_____

_____

Germany's Secret Code

_____

_____

_____

_____

Many Ways to Communicate

American Sign Language

_____

_____

_____

_____

Morse Code

_____

_____

_____

_____

2. Choose two systems for communicating that you read about in this topic. Tell how they are alike and different.

_____

_____

_____

_____

3. Why is it important to be able to communicate in more than one way?

_____

_____

_____

_____

4. How would you explain to a friend what you learned in this topic?

_____

_____

_____

_____

Comics and Cartoons

In comics, speech balloons show what people say or think.

Fast Facts

- In Italy, comic strips are named "little puffs of smoke" because of the speech balloons.

- By 1938, readers could find war and Superman® comic strips in their newspapers.

- A filmmaker paid $1 million for the first Superman comic book.

The Comic Strip

American comic strips first appeared in New York City at the end of the 19th century. At that time, a newspaper called[25] the *New York World* began running a comic strip called "The Yellow Kid," which many people think was the first comic in the[48] United States. "The Yellow Kid" got its name because his clothes were colored with yellow ink. "The Yellow Kid" had speech[69] balloons that showed the words people spoke. Soon, almost every newspaper printed comics, or funnies, as they are also called.[89]

Today, comic strips, many with speech balloons, are found in newspapers across the country. On Sundays, the color comics[108] are one of the most popular parts of the newspaper. In addition, the Sunday comics are usually larger and more colorful than the daily comics.[133]

KEY NOTES

The Comic Strip
What was "The Yellow Kid"?

_____

_____

Comics and Cartoons

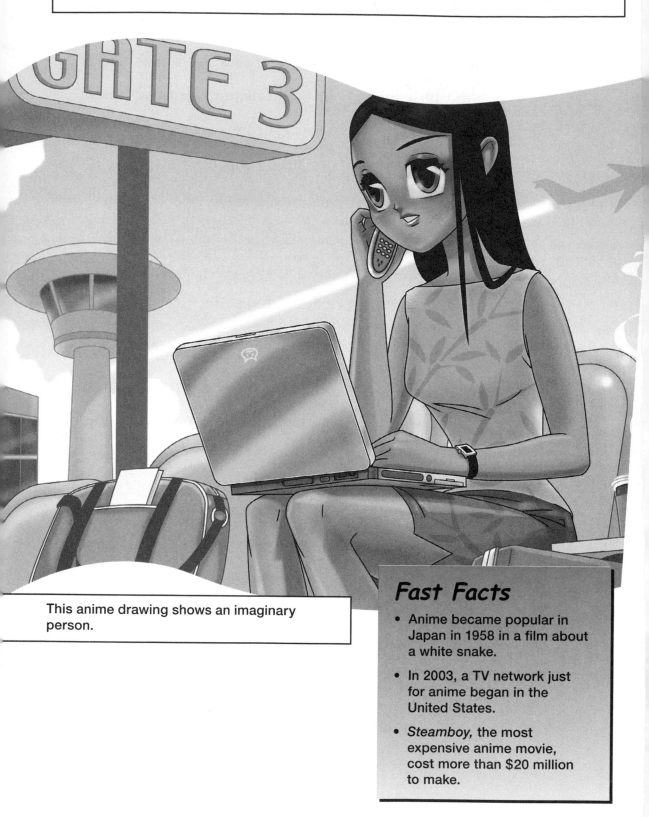

This anime drawing shows an imaginary person.

Fast Facts

- Anime became popular in Japan in 1958 in a film about a white snake.

- In 2003, a TV network just for anime began in the United States.

- *Steamboy,* the most expensive anime movie, cost more than $20 million to make.

Anime

In Japan, people of all ages read anime and watch it on TV and in movies. Anime is the name of a style of art and cartoon[28] that was created in Japan in the 1950s. The anime that people read and watch in the United States often features children and imaginary beasts that have huge eyes.[57]

Since anime films and TV shows were first created, their viewers have grown up. Although Japanese viewers still love[76] the anime style of drawing, they now want stories that feature adults. Many anime books, films, and TV shows are still created[98] for children, but now there are anime love stories and sports tales, too. Some anime also features fighting and imaginary[118] worlds. In addition, anime movies are being made of classic Japanese films.[130]

KEY NOTES

Anime

How has anime changed over the years?

_____

_____

Comics and Cartoons

This person is dressed like a science fiction character in a graphic novel.

Fast Facts

- Graphic novels are becoming a strong part of book sales, with $120 million in sales in 2003.

- The first modern graphic novel was published in 1978.

- One famous graphic novel is 6,000 pages long.

Graphic Novels

Although they don't look like novels, they also don't look like comic books. Graphic novels, which look like a mixture of comics and novels, are an art form that blends fiction and art.[35]

Graphic novels look like comic books because they have drawings and tell stories. However, they are different from[53] comics because they tell longer stories that are more like those told in novels. Also like novels, they may have many characters and a plot with many parts.[81]

Both teens and adults enjoy graphic novels' strong drawings and stories. In addition, graphic novels feature many[98] different subjects. Some graphic novelists write about World War II. Some write love stories or science fiction. Others write[117] stories that make readers laugh. Graphic novels today appeal to a growing number of readers.[132]

KEY NOTES
Graphic Novels What are graphic novels? _____ _____

Comics and Cartoons

Computer animation lets artists draw real-looking cartoons.

Fast Facts

- The first animated film, about funny faces, was made in 1906.

- Computers that are used for animation can be 100 times faster than most home computers.

- A computer-animated film can take from one to five years to make.

Computer Animation

Before computers, hundreds of artists spent years carefully drawing frame after frame to make an animated film. Every[20] second of film needed 12 to 24 drawings. A five-minute cartoon could have more than 7,000 drawings.[38]

Today, most animated films are drawn on computers. Computer animation can look almost as real as life. The animals[57] seem to move like real animals, even though they can talk. The people look more real, too, even though they can stretch[79] like clay. Some films also combine real people and animals with computer animation.[92]

The film *Toy Story*, which was first shown in 1995, was the first full-length computer-animated film, and it was very[114] popular. Today, many artists who once drew each frame by hand now create cartoons with computer animation.[131]

KEY NOTES

Computer Animation
What is computer animation?

_____

_____

Comics and Cartoons

The Comic Strip

1. "The Comic Strip" is MAINLY about _____

    a. "The Yellow Kid."
    b. comic strips in newspapers.
    c. newspapers in the 19th century.
    d. how speech balloons changed the comics.

2. Another name for comics in newspapers is _____

    a. the funnies.
    b. Yellow Kids.
    c. Sunday strips.
    d. speech balloons.

3. What are speech balloons?

_____

_____

_____

Anime

1. What is anime?

_____

_____

_____

2. Another good name for "Anime" is _____

    a. "Japanese Art."
    b. "Comics in the 1950s."
    c. "Comics Around the World."
    d. "Cartoons From Japan."

3. Why is anime now drawn for adults, too?

_____

_____

_____

Graphic Novels

1. The main idea of "Graphic Novels" is that _____

    a. graphic novels blend comics and fiction.
    b. graphic novels are the same as comic strips.
    c. comic-book artists draw graphic novels.
    d. graphic novels take much longer for artists to draw.

2. In this reading, *graphic* means _____

    a. related to cartoons
    b. related to drawing
    c. related to novels
    d. related to a style of drawing

3. How are graphic novels and comics alike and different?

_____

_____

_____

Computer Animation

1. What does *animated* mean in this reading?

    a. made from comic books
    b. made to look like an animal
    c. made with computers
    d. made to look alive

2. How was animation first created?

_____

_____

_____

3. How did computers change animated films?

_____

_____

_____

comics	balloons	anime	imaginary
graphic novel	fiction	animated	computer

1. Choose the word from the word box above that best matches each definition. Write the word on the line below.

A. _____ a machine that is used to store and use information

B. _____ not real

C. _____ writing that does not show real people or events

D. _____ a type of long story that uses fiction and art

E. _____ bags filled with air that float in the sky

F. _____ a style of art created in Japan

G. _____ drawings, often with words, that may tell a story

H. _____ made to seem alive

2. Fill in the blanks in the sentences below. Choose the word from the word box that completes each sentence.

A. The _____ style of art was first created in Japan.

B. Speech _____ show the words cartoon characters are saying.

C. Some artists create _____ animals that never existed on Earth.

D. I like to read the _____ strips in the newspaper.

E. _____ films often have talking animals.

F. Today, an artist can use a _____ to create animated films quickly.

G. Juan liked reading _____ about people living on other worlds.

H. The _____ looked like a comic book, but its story was much longer.

Comics and Cartoons

1. Use the idea web to help you remember what you read. In each box, write the main idea of that reading.

The Comic Strip

_____

_____

_____

_____

Anime

_____

_____

_____

Comics and Cartoons

Graphic Novels

_____

_____

_____

Computer Animation

_____

_____

_____

2. How have comics and cartoons changed?

_____

_____

_____

_____

3. How are comic strips, anime, and computer animation similar?

_____

_____

_____

_____

4. Tell about your favorite form of comics or cartoons and why you like it.

_____

_____

_____

_____

Acknowledgments

Photo Credits

Cover photos: (top) BananaStock/Punchstock; (bottom, L-R) Stockbyte Silver/Getty Images; Comstock Images/Punchstock; Digital Vision/ Punchstock; Dave Bartruff/Digital Vision/ Getty Images; **Page:** 8 © Amy Etra/PhotoEdit; 10 © Michael Newman/PhotoEdit; 12 Special Olympics; 14 © Michael Newman/PhotoEdit; 22 AP Images; 24 Andrew Rafkind/Getty Images; 26 Haruyoshi Yamguchi /Corbis; 28 © Stringer/Malaysia/Reuters/Corbis; 36 Herral Long Photographer; 38 3M; 40 © Spencer Grant/ PhotoEdit; 42 David Parker/Science Museum/ Science Photo Library/Photo Researchers, Inc.; 50 Sena Vidanagama/AFP/Getty Images; 52 Michael Medford/The Image Bank/Getty Images; 54 The Art Archive/Private Collection/Dagli Orti; 56 © Robbie Jack/Corbis; 64 American Photographer (20th Century)/Private Collection/ Peter Newark American Pictures/The Bridgeman Art Library; 66 Frank Driggs Collection; 68 © Lloyd Wolf/Lebrecht; 70 © JazzSign/Lebrecht; 78 © Bettmann/Corbis; 80 © Corbis; 82 Library of Congress; 84 Kathy Willens/Associated Press; 92 © Stephen Coburn/Shutterstock; 94 © Craig Aurness/Corbis. All Rights Reserved.; 96 © Brooks Kraft/Corbis. All Rights Reserved.; 98 Lester Sloan/Woodfin Camp & Associates; 106 Donald E. Carroll/The Image Bank/Getty Images; 108 National Oceanic and Atmospheric Administration; 110 Jeff Hunter/Photographer's Choice/Getty Images; 112 Gary Vestal/Stone/ Getty Images; 120, 122 The Art Archive/Dagli Orti; 124 The Art Archive/Pharaonic Village, Cairo/Dagli Orti; 126 © Mike Howell/SuperStock, Inc.; 134 Martin Westlake/Asia Images/Getty Images; 136, 138 The Granger Collection, New York; 140 Wally Herbert/Robert Harding; 148 Rex Interstock/The Stock Connection; 150 Volker Steger/Photo Researchers, Inc.; 152 © Myrleen Ferguson Cate/PhotoEdit; 154 © Cindy Charles/ PhotoEdit; 162 Reproduced by Peaco Todd; 164 © Creatas/SuperStock; 166 © Syracuse Newspapers/ David Lassman/The Image Works; 168 Markus Matzel/Peter Arnold, Inc.

Text Credits

- Kevlar® is a registered trademark of DuPont™.
- *The Lion King*. Copyright © The Walt Disney Company.
- *The Mummy*. Copyright © 1999 Universal Studios. All rights reserved.
- *Adrift: Seventy Six Days Lost at Sea* by Steven Callahan. Copyright © 1986, 1999 by Steven Callahan. All rights reserved. New York: Houghton Mifflin/Mariner Books.
- *Jaws* by Peter Benchley. Copyright © 1974 by Peter Benchley. Published by The Random House Publishing Group. New York: Random House/Fawcett.
- *The Call of the Wild* and *White Fang* by Jack London. Copyright © 2004. New York: Sterling Publishing Co., Inc.
- *Enigma*. Copyright © 2002 Manhattan Pictures International LLC.
- *Superman*®. Copyright © DC Comics. All Rights Reserved.
- *Steamboy*. 1994. Dir. Katsuhiro Ôtomo. © 2005 Katsuhiro Ôtomo-Mashroom/Steamboy Committee. All Rights Reserved.
- *Toy Story*. 1995. Dir. John Lasseter. A Pixar Production. Unless expressly authorized in writing by the copyright owner, any copying, exhibition, export, distribution or other use of this product or any part of it is strictly prohibited. Distributed by Buena Vista Home Entertainment, Inc., Dept. CS, Burbank, CA 91521. Printed in USA. © 1995 Walt Disney Company; *Toy Story 2* Copyright © Disney Enterprises, Inc./Pixar Animation Studios.

Staff Credits

Members of the AMP™ QReads™ team: Melania Benzinger, Karen Blonigen, Carol Bowling, Michelle Carlson, Kazuko Collins, Nancy Condon, Barbara Drewlo, Sue Gulsvig, Daren Hastings, Laura Henrichsen, Ruby Hogen-Chin, Julie Johnston, Mary Kaye Kuzma, Julie Maas, Daniel Milowski, Carrie O'Connor, Julie Theisen, Mary Verrill, Mike Vineski, Charmaine Whitman